SPIRITUAL RENEWAL

The Pain and the Glory

LAMAR VEST

Pathway
P·R·E·S·S
CLEVELAND, TENNESSEE 37311

The **Pain** and the **Glory**

ISBN: 0-87148-813-2

Library of Congress Catalog Card Number: 88-061513

Copyright © 1988
PATHWAY PRESS
Cleveland, Tennessee 37311

Printed in the United States of America

Contents

3. Our Minds Seem Confused
Renewal of Concepts _____

We are more image-oriented today than we are concept-oriented. We seem more concerned with acceptance than with accuracy. The idea that success breeds success leads us to strive for immediate results more than for long-lasting effects.

4. We Are Each Responsible
Renewal of the Personal Life _____

The path to spiritual death is so natural and easy we scarcely realize it is happening. It begins when we deliberately suppress truth or refuse to receive it.

5. Much More Is Needed
Renewal of the Corporate Body_____

For many years I have believed that if enough individuals become involved in personal renewal, the corporate renewal of the church would be automatic. I no longer believe that. Like Israel, the Body must make a corporate move toward God.

Dedication

This book is gratefully dedicated to those who have shaped my theology and clarified the Bible principles by which I live; to those who have listened to me hour after hour, sharing my burdens, dreams and hopes for the future of this church; and to all those special friends in the ministry whose personalities have blended into what I now recognize as a priceless religious heritage.

"A church that has lost its purity or its sense of vitality in ministry is totally useless in bringing the power and truth of the gospel to this world."

Introduction

A few months ago the residents of Cleveland, Tennessee, were startled by an earthquake. Most, except perhaps those of us who had lived in California, did not realize what had happened. There was a jolting noise which sounded something like a sonic boom. The swaying chandeliers and a strange sensation that the earth was moving, however, indicated that something more was happening.

An article in the afternoon newspaper explained that we had, in fact, experienced a genuine earthquake. The article further revealed that Memphis, Tennessee, is in danger of an earthquake which could possibly be more devastating than the long-anticipated California earthquake. California has built for a possible earthquake. Memphis has not.

The **Pain** and the **Glory**

Among my first thoughts was a spiritual application. I wondered, "Is today's church able to withstand a shaking of the Holy Spirit?" There will be an occasional shaking. It is absolutely necessary for the ongoing mission and purity of the church. A righteous God will not permit His church to drift into disrespect for His Word and lose sight of its mission. His judgment will expose sin in the church and His Holy Spirit will call the faithful to a spiritual renewal.

We are living in a day of great transition. We are actually watching the collapse of the world as we have known it. It is obvious to the most casual observer that our political and economic systems are becoming increasingly ineffective. The very values that have shaped our society are being discarded like last year's bird's nest. The global challenges of war, famine and human indignities are pushing our civilization to the brink of despair.

What happens when we place the church in the middle of such diverse and complex circumstances? Is today's church capable of facing the challenges of a dying world? Or is it possible that we have not yet even felt the slackening pulse beat of this old world and therefore are unaware of its condition? Perhaps the real question is "Can our kind of church save our kind of world?"

I am convinced that God's church is capable of ministry to any generation. I am equally convinced, however, that a church which has lost its purity or its sense of vitality in ministry is totally useless in bringing the power and truth of the gospel to this world. Thus, God periodically breaks in upon His people with a call to renewal. A positive response to that call delivers the church from sin and frees it of fatigue, despair and cynicism. It is only when the church sees clearly its SPIRITUAL relationship to a holy God and holds its mission in constant focus that it is able to act purposefully and meaningfully. Only a church which acts from this base of choice and intent will be a positive force in today's world.

Throughout history God's people have been brought face-to-face with great opportunities for spiritual awakenings. It is still happening today. Some of us look straight at these opportunities and walk away. Why? We are either living on prejudice or in ignorance. Either we have already made up our minds what we will permit God to do in our lives and have no intentions of changing, or we are ignorant of God's will and power to move within our totally human experience.

Renewal is not merely another priority of the church. It is essential, an absolute. We will either submit to God's refinement and respond positively to it, or we will face the stern alternative of exile where God will meet us afresh in the wilderness to lead us with pain and glory into the promised inheritance.

Lamar Vest
Cleveland, Tennessee

"Unless the real issues facing the church are dealt with, and unless the hurts, questions and pains of the Body are fully expressed and embraced, there will be no renewal."

1
Something Is Wrong

The whole idea of renewal in the church is predicated upon the belief that all is not well. If, indeed, everything is as it should be, there is no need for reform and renewal. Too many want to have renewal without ever understanding and admitting that something is wrong.

There are many struggles in today's church. We face the challenge of defining and committing to a structure that will move the Church of God with exacting momentum into its second century of ministry. We are dealing with a financial crisis that threatens to bring about radical changes in ministry priorities. A lack of personal and corporate commitment endangers the fulfillment of our calling, and a prevailing leadership crisis implies a limit to our future growth. A crisis in faith and doctrine poses serious questions for many as to what it is that actually constitutes church membership. Broken relationships suggest a spoiling of the church's unity. The uncertainty of mission has prompted some to become involved in frenzied and sometimes dangerous activities in the name of church growth.

Unless the real issues facing the church are dealt with, and unless the hurts, questions and pains of the Body are fully expressed and embraced, there will be no renewal. Jesus would have never wept for Jerusalem unless He knew that all was not well. Illness cannot be cured until it is diagnosed. God is free to heal us only when we acknowledge we need healing.

For sometime I have had a growing conviction that God is calling the church to renewal such as we have never experienced. The prevailing feeling seems to be that we are either facing our finest hour or that we may be stymied in our growth and remembered historically as a movement which got sidetracked somewhere from an opportunity for greatness. It is not enough for us to applaud the past. Nor can we become so bound to the past that we cannot accept a fresh move of the Holy Spirit today. We must examine our past, review our present fulfillment of mission and determine what story we will write for the future. It would be a great tragedy if the Church of God failed to live up to its calling. It would be an even greater tragedy to lose forever those treasures which have been passed to us by godly men and women.

If we can own up to our failure and needs before a holy God (Isaiah 6), and if we submit to His holy refinement, then I believe our future as a church is one of great hope and bright promise. The birthplace of all genuine spiritual renewal is in the presence of God's holiness. Unless we have a view of a holy God we have no idea what we are moving toward.

Renewal is more than church growth, furious activity or a surface change in structure. It is more than moving furniture around and rearranging decor. Some churches have altered the format of their worship services, replaced the pulpit with a stool, eliminated Sunday school and called it renewal. Spiritual renewal can only be defined in terms of purity, pathos and mission.

Renewal is costly. As Charles Swindoll said in comparing renewal to the remodeling of a home:

1. It takes longer than you planned.

2. It costs more than you figured.

3. It is messier than you anticipated.

4. It requires greater determination than you expected (*Strike the Original Match*, 1980, p. 10).

Larry Christenson has said, "...A renewal movement does not bring something *new* in an absolute sense. On the contrary, it seeks to bring the church in line with a truth older than that by which it is presently living. It addresses unchanging truth to a changed time. It is a corrective, not a new norm " (*Welcome Holy Spirit*, 1987, p. 36).

Spiritual renewal is a dynamic happening. It is a vibrant movement brought about by an act of the Holy Spirit. It will never come through human efforts. If that were possible, renewal would be perpetual in the church. Somewhere we seem to have gotten the idea that if we can get the right people working on any problem, they will eventually come up with a workable solution. Thus, an inordinate amount of our time and energy is taken up with those things that cannot possibly awaken the church or change the world. We have spent more time in recent years reviewing our organizational structure than Jesus Christ devoted to His entire ministry on earth. Yet very little has changed.

It is noteworthy that none of the great spiritual awakenings of the past were started by a group of ecclesiastical leaders who called a conference and announced, "Now let's get busy and have a spiritual awakening." Quite contrary to that, spiritual awakenings are ushered in by simple people who get so hungry for a move of God they can't eat, sleep or be content until they experience a fresh, explosive move of God. Our plans and programs may help get us in the right frame of mind and spirit, but they will never bring about renewal. Renewal is a gift of God to desperate, spiritually hungry people.

One of the great dangers in religion is that it will become dead and formalistic, without the genuine touch of God. Formalism induces dullness to spiritual matters. It robs people of the passions associated with fervent devotion to God and deprives them of being God's people on earth. Formality and ritualism lead eventually to bored, sad, tired churches that can never be channels for fresh outpourings of the Holy Spirit.

Formalism was a chief sin of ancient Israel. The Israelites became so perfunctory in their religious ceremony that they forgot the original object of their worship. They forgot the glorious deliverance from Egypt and the marvelous preservation of God in the wilderness. They forgot the covenants they had made with God. In perhaps their greatest act of ingratitude, they created their own substitutes for God, prompting Jeremiah to cry out:

Hath a nation changed their gods, which are yet no gods? but my people have changed their glory for that which doth not profit. Be astonished, O ye heavens, at this, and be horribly afraid, be ye very desolate, saith the Lord. For my people have committed two evils; they have forsaken me the fountain of living waters, and hewed them out cisterns, broken cisterns, that can hold no water (Jeremiah 2:11-13).

Inherent in any religious movement are the possibilities that it can become institutionalized and lose its vitality. Methodism was still a very young movement when John Wesley expressed concerns over the potential danger that it could degenerate into a mere sect, losing its commitment to the centrality of God's Word and its evangelistic fervor. Wesley knew what most of us recognize today: Movements can grow stale. Movements, organizations and institutions help us find God, but sometimes they become the very hindrances that keep us from knowing the mind of God. This is especially true of second- and third-generation movements, for as people grow older there is danger of mistaking *form* for *force* and consequently a deterioration of calling and purpose.

Periodically, within any church, the seeds of renewal and reformation must be resown and cultivated. The crust of formality and ritualism must be pierced in order that individuals might connect personally in relationship with God. Sometimes dissatisfaction, disappointments and discouragements are God's way of getting our attention for renewal.

The founding fathers of the Church of God viewed themselves as advocates of renewal. Seeing their churches departing from biblical patterns, they called for a renewal from within which never came. They did not leave their denominations by choice. They were forced out. R. G. Spurling Jr. wrote a little booklet shortly after the turn of the century in which he shared the agony of separation from his church. He wrote:

> They demanded my license which I readily gave up, hoping that I could preach what I saw the Bible to teach instead of what some other man believed....Now I must forever quit preaching or leave my church, so I left them, choosing to obey God rather than man. Here it seemed to me that my little boat must forever sink as I was turned out of what I once thought was Christ's only true church.

When the Church of God was born more than 100 years ago, it was not known whether it would live or die. The possibilities were more in favor of an early death than on the side of survival. God chose to let that embryonic church live. It has withstood many storms and battles, both internally and externally. Its weak voice was unheard at first, but now the Church of God has become a respected voice which is being heard around the world. The question is, now that we are being heard, are we saying the right

"Formality and ritualism lead eventually to bored, sad, tired churches which can never be channels for fresh outpourings of the Holy Spirit."

things?

How do the seeds of renewal planted by those early church fathers relate to a movement that has now entered into its second century of ministry? We minister in a world enamored by largeness and power, whose theme song has become "Gimme That Big-Time Religion." People are influenced not as much by truth as they are by super churches, charismatic personalities and a new-wave gospel. It is especially important at this time in our history that we look seriously at the mission God raised us up to fulfill.

Ironically new moves of God are usually rejected and sometimes opposed by those who were part of a previous spiritual awakening. We should never forget the role of the Pharisees in preserving the tenets of Judaism, thus preparing the way for the Messiah to be born. Yet, as we know, the Pharisees became our Lord's greatest enemies.

The Roman Catholic Church held forth the truths of God for centuries but fought the Reformation of Luther. The Lutherans were among the greatest opponents of the Wesleyan revival. Out of Wesleyanism came the Holiness Movement, which was rejected by Methodism as a whole. From the Holiness Movement, around the turn of the century, came the modern-day Pentecostal Movement. And who were among the greatest fighters of Pentecostalism? The very people who were involved in the holiness awakening. God forbid that the Pentecostal Movement should ever be guilty of fighting or opposing anything God wishes to do in this generation.

Sometimes a new movement challenges and convicts us of our own ineptitude and ineffectiveness. We know if we accept the challenge of spiritual renewal we may have to radically change our lives. We are too comfortable for that, too adjusted to a lifestyle that seems adequate to keep us out of hell. When opportunities for renewal come our way, we either meet them with openness or we walk away, resisting the very thing that will bring us into contact with a fresh move of God's Holy Spirit.

If we are to respond positively to God's call to renewal, several things must happen. Perhaps by reviewing a few of them our hearts will be opened to a fresh move of God.

TRUE SPIRITUAL RENEWAL IS PRECEDED BY CONFESSION AND REPENTANCE

It has become popular for us to blame the world for our problems, but the judgment of God is being focused on the church, not on the world. The Bible says, "The time is come that judgment must begin at the house of God" (1 Peter 4:17). It is time we acknowledge that we don't suffer from the sins of the world as much as we do from the sins of the church. Whether we like it or not, God has ordained the solidarity of the Body. The principle of shared guilt is always present. Paul tells us in 1 Corinthians 12:26 that when "one member suffer[s], all the members suffer with it." When one member harbors sins, the whole body is affected. A little cold water will lower the temperature of the whole body.

God is no respecter of sin. It doesn't matter whether you tell a lie in a barroom or a church choir—if you lie,

19

you're a liar. It doesn't matter whether you get drunk in overalls or a tuxedo—when you get drunk, you are a drunkard. Extramarital relations in the church are as much adultery and sin as those in the world. Hate, prejudice and injustice are as much sin to the church member as to the infidel, and the only way sin can be dealt with is through confession and repentance. Charles Finney warned, "Christians are more to blame for not being revived than sinners are for not being saved."

David Watson says in *I Believe in the Church,* "Unless renewal precedes evangelism, the credibility gap between what the church *preaches* and what the church *is* will be too wide to be bridged. It is only when the world sees the living body of Christ on earth that it will be in any way convinced of the reality and relevance of Christ himself" (1978, p. 18).

How can we expect the world to know the love of Christ if we Christians don't love each other? How can we hope to change the world if the world doesn't see a change in us?

SPIRITUAL RENEWAL IS PRECEDED BY A STATE OF SPIRITUAL BROKENNESS

God's covenants with man have always been born of a broken spirit which cries out to God as the only source of hope and healing. God said to the Israelites, "I have surely seen the affliction of my people which are in Egypt, and have heard their cry by reason of their taskmasters; for I know their sorrows; And I am come down to deliver them out of the hand of the Egyptians, and to bring them up out of that land unto a good land and a large, unto a land flowing with milk and honey" (Exodus 3:7, 8). God is drawn to the contrite and broken heart.

So much of our religious activity today speaks of a surface devotion. Noticeably absent is the pathos portrayed in the spiritual awakenings of the past. We speak of our faith in terms of an easy-come, easy-go religion that is not meant to seriously affect our daily lives. A prevailing view among many Christians seems to be that "religion is OK as long as it doesn't get in the way of how we live." True faith in God *will* get in the way of how we live. The true people of God cannot look upon human needs, social injustices and the lost state of man without being broken.

Christianity is a corporate experience. We need each other, and we are greatly influenced by one another. When one hurts, we all hurt. When one is revived, there is the potential of sparking a revival in all of us. We must all share in the pain of renewal. None can be exempt. Regardless of what comfortable position we may have attained in life or in our Christian service, not one of us can avoid feeling the pain of our brothers and sisters who are in need. The secret of our extraordinary fellowship has been our shared passions. If there are no shared passions, there can be no shared friendships.

SPIRITUAL RENEWAL IS PRECEDED BY AN EXTRAORDINARY BURDEN FOR PRAYER

Jonathan Edwards said, "When God has something very great for His church, it is His will that there should precede it the extraordinary prayers of His people." History certainly bears record to this truth. I have never heard of renewal that was not ushered in by praying people.

For the most part, we are convinced that prayer is important and necessary. But prayer continues to be more praised than practiced. If as many people prayed as talked about prayer, what a different world this would be. Most casualties of the spiritual life can be traced back to the place of weakened prayer life. Over and again prayer has accounted for victory in the memoirs of God's people. Many Christians have risen above difficult circumstances by power tapped through earnest prayer. Prayer has opened the door for great accomplishments for the church. The "effectual fervent prayer of a righteous man" (James 5:16) still avails much.

Presently, more emphasis is being placed on prayer than at any time I can remember. This is a positive indicator that renewal is on the way. The rewards of prayer are unlimited: "Unto him that is able to do exceeding abundantly above all that we ask or think, according to the power that worketh in us" (Ephesians 3:20).

SPIRITUAL RENEWAL IS PRECEDED BY A PASSION FOR RIGHTEOUSNESS

Too many Christians have had their passion for things of God dulled by a lust for the secular. The things they see, touch, drive or put in the bank have come to mean more to them than the things of God. The Bible says of ancient Judah, "[They made no] difference between the holy and the profane" (Ezekiel 44:23). We must have a revival of the sacred. We must place greater emphasis on pleasing God than on fulfilling our own ambitions.

Regardless of how the world stretches its moral values to accommodate selfish and erotic desires, God's people can never tolerate unholy things. There can be no detente with the world. If the world moves in, the church becomes comfortable and compromising, and such a church is powerless to combat the evils of this day.

Someone recently used a term that hit me hard. They referred to some religious groups today who are promoting "cheap grace." There is no such thing. The two words can't even be used in the same breath. If it is cheap, it isn't grace at all. If it is grace, it can never be called cheap. Those who have been redeemed by the precious blood of Jesus Christ have been saved from sin. We have been freed from the enslavement of Satan. We have been admitted to the secrets of God's pavilion, and we share with Him in all His plans for the future. That is not cheap. Grace always demands a life which reflects the glory of Him who redeemed us by His precious grace.

SPIRITUAL AWAKENINGS ARE ALWAYS PRECEDED BY A RENEWED COMMITMENT TO MISSION

An organization which has lost sight of its mission is as good as dead. No amount of professionalism, energy or creative genius will ever cover for a group of people who have lost their reason for being.

Several years ago I was approached by a lady in a

church where I visited and asked to purchase a dozen doughnuts.

As I reached for my money I asked, "Do you mind telling me why you are selling doughnuts?"

"Not at all," she responded. "Right now we are having to buy doughnuts from a bakery, so we are raising money to build our own kitchen so we can make our own doughnuts."

Somewhere in this whole process somebody lost sight of the mission.

George Santayana once said, "Fanaticism is redoubling your efforts when you have forgotten your aim." If that is true, then I'm afraid fanaticism abounds in many churches. Far too much church work centers solely on keeping lights on and the bills paid, or living up to some reputation, or making our church buildings bigger and better than those across town. While maintenance of our churches is obviously necessary, something has gone pathetically wrong when maintenance becomes an end in itself.

God raised up the Church of God as a Word-centered movement. The very first principle adopted by those early members was "The Church of God stands for the whole Bible rightly divided. The New Testament is the only rule for government and discipline." The day we abandon that mission is the very day we lose our purpose for existence. The church must always see its main mission as preaching and teaching the Word of God, not as defined by our own interpretation but as the verbal inspiration of God. We do not have a choice as to which part of the Bible we will believe or reject. We are

"Unfortunately, much of our preaching and teaching today is centered on how to get our act together rather than on how to get in on God's act."

committed to all that God's Word says.

Unfortunately, much of our preaching and teaching is centered on how to get our act together rather than on how to get in on God's act. We talk about how much God loves us and how He wants to help us make it through the day. This is all good and true, but where is the blazing light of the risen Christ? Where is the message of repentance, conversion, purity and commitment?

Our mission is threatened when our preaching and teaching center more on current issues and personal problems than on the Word. We violate our mission when we concentrate more on an analysis of our needs than on celebrating the history of God and His dealings with man. There is evidently a crisis in theology when men are more concerned about being accepted and respected than they are in taking unpopular stands for God's truth.

Our mission is threatened when we put personal interests ahead of what God has called us to do. Ours is a self-seeking society. So much of what this society does comes out of a "what's in it for me" mentality. Walter Brueggemann says, "The primary ideological voices of our time are the voices of autonomy: to do one's own thing, self-actualization, self-assertion, self-fulfillment. The ideology of our time is to propose that one can live an 'uncalled life,' one not referred to any purpose beyond one's self." (*Hopeful Imagination*, 1986, p. 19). A nation cannot exist without statesmen. How much more important it is for a church to have churchmen, men who will put God's work above their own interests!

I shall never forget the 1960 General Assembly in

Memphis, Tennessee. It was not an earthquaking issue before the General Council but one that allowed a true churchman to speak. The issue was whether or not we should change the name of the Supreme Council to the Executive Council. R. P. Johnson was hardly able to stand when he walked to the microphone and said, "Brethren, there is no one supreme to God. We are robbing God of His glory. We are but men. We are not supreme." The name was changed.

The Church of God was raised up to be an evangelistic church. From the very beginning, the church has accepted the challenge of being part of fulfilling the Great Commission of Jesus Christ. Its evangelism challenge has taken it to all states, to most countries of the world and to people of various national origins. Our mission is threatened when we become discriminating in our evangelistic outreach, eliminating any group because of race or economic status. God raised us up to reach every person we can with the full truth of His Word. Our message is to every human being regardless of race, color or economic status. Bertha Condes' Paraphrasing of Isaiah 61 is a very relevant and poignant warning to today's church:

> *The Spirit of God is upon me, one of the privileged class of a long line of ancestors. He gives me the exalted career of preaching good news to the best families in our town; ours is the most representative and leading church. He sent me to release all resources from those who have every advantage and to illumine with new inspirations those who have been in the church*

The **Pain** and the **Glory**

for years. I came to build a magnificent building to replace the small, uncomfortable church we have had. Our goal is to use all publicity in order to bring into our fold great numbers of desirable people so that we may retain our place as the most influential church in the city.

The mission of the Church of God is a Pentecostal mission. It is still a mystery to many as to why God would choose to pour out His Holy Spirit on those simple believers in the Unicoi Mountains of eastern Tennessee and western North Carolina. We may never understand the why, but we do know that it did happen. It is therefore incumbent upon us to be a clarion voice in Christendom for the Holy Spirit baptism. We can neither avoid addressing that segment of Christianity which denies the baptism of the Holy Spirit nor those Charismatics who are open to the Spirit baptism although they may not have a full understanding of other doctrines which accompany it. The Holy Spirit rejects narrowness. He will not be limited in His work by the prejudices and inflexibilities of man.

The Church of God was raised up to be a voice for purity and righteousness. Our roots are deeply planted in the Holiness Movement, and we must never abandon that heritage. We must possess a passion for righteousness which speaks out against the ungodly and profane wherever they are found.

Nothing brings more shame to the church than does the loss of moral and ethical purity. God has so clearly stated His standard for living that there can be no question

28

as to whether holiness in life is an option or a requirement. When those who claim to be His people live in such way as to contradict God's Word, God is grieved and His work on earth is greatly hindered. He will not tolerate lack of purity on the part of those who name the name of Christ.

The church must be awakened to the challenge of our day. The life and health of the nation and the world depend upon the spiritual health of the church. There will never be a change in the world until there is a change in the church. The world cannot limit the Holy Spirit. Only the church can do that.

The life of the church is in its roots. I believe God is calling the church to return to its roots, not to dig up and attempt to transplant the vine to some other vineyard. There isn't enough time for another movement to be raised up to do what God has called the Church of God to do. We are certainly not the only movement through which God has chosen to work; but never doubt we were raised up for a specific mission, and as long as we fulfill that purpose all hell will not prevail against us. If we cease to fulfill our mission, it will not take hell to destroy us. We will destroy ourselves.

The winds of revival are blowing again. People who would not even listen a few years ago are now open to the Word. God help us not to sleep through this renewal. Whether the faith of our fathers degenerates into the creed of our children depends on how successful we are in remaining true to our reason for being. The world has witnessed our shame and our failures. Let us now show them God in the midst of His people.

If God has been dealing with you about renewal,

about revival, about restoration of our founding principles, please do more than talk about it. If you don't approve of all that is taking place in the church, don't resort to cynicism or a critical spirit. Become an instrument of His righteousness to bring about a great spiritual awakening that will clearly identify us as God's people on this earth.

———————————

Principles
of
Renewal

1
Spiritual Brokenness

2
Confession and Repentance

3
Burden for Prayer

4
Passion for Righteousness

5
Commitment to Mission

"When a church loses the ability to be moved by the burdens of others, to be outraged at the work of evil or to feel indignant at the injustices of society, its love has turned to apathy."

2

WE DON'T SEEM TO CARE

Someone spoke recently of a couple whose marriage of 15 years had become a "tired friendship." It doesn't take long for the mere routine of religious activity to lose its vitality and to degenerate into a sort of tired friendship. As William James has said, "Religion is either a dull habit or an acute fever."

Many Christians have lost their burning passion for God. Whatever freshness and excitement they once experienced has been lost. Thousands of regular church-goers are suffering from the "religious blahs." Old songs have lost their meaning. Past experiences have become faded memories of days they are not even sure ever existed. Even some ministers have lost the exciting edge that once pressed them into Christian service. One minister recently defined a sermon as something you would go around the world to preach but wouldn't cross the street to hear.

A weariness of spirit is obvious among many of God's people. Much of our conversation centers around being tired, overcommitted or on the fringe of burnout. Too many Christians are going through the motions of serving God. They feel trapped: too afraid of hell to dump God altogether but too overwhelmed by the agony and pain of a dying world to really believe they can actually make a difference. The only thing that can possibly restore them to vitality of spirit, to where they see Christianity as a spiritual adventure rather than a perfunctory service, is to arise from the morass of the apathetic and be renewed in their relationship with a sovereign God.

The sovereignty of God is our most powerful source of hope. God is not defeated. He has not vacated His throne. He is not absent from this earth. He has not given up on us. He is near and available to all who will yield to His will. A renewed vision of God is essential to a renewed awareness of our position as His people.

Apathy goes to the root of today's moral and spiritual crises. It is the thief of renewal. It takes bread from the mouths of the hungry and deprives the thirsty of the fresh waters of God's deep fountains. It condemns men and women to a life of separation from God and robs God's people of a daily, vibrant relationship with Him. It keeps God's church in a state of catatonic slumber and reduces it to nothing more than a social order.

The English word *apathy* comes from the Greek word *apatheia* , which means without passion, or the absence of pathos. God has ordained that the church love people and have compassion in meeting their needs. When a church loses the ability to be moved by the burdens of others, to be outraged at the work of evil or to feel indignant at the injustices of society, its love has turned to apathy. The greatest motivation for our compassion toward others is an understanding that the only reason we exist and survive is because of God's concern for us.

How can we, for whom God has done so much, ever shut our eyes and hearts to the needs of others? Stuart Briscoe says, "The compassion of God...it is the very basis of our existence, our redemption, our survival. Understanding this, we should look into our own hearts and see whether something of that nature has been imparted to us by the Holy Spirit. Put in the simplest terms: if I have tasted compassion, am I disseminating it?" (*How to Be a Motivated Christian,* 1987, p. 87).

In Matthew 18, Jesus shares one of the most impactful stories of His ministry. It is about a man who owed his superior a great debt he could not pay. So he fell down before his creditor and begged for compassion. He was immediately forgiven, and his ledger was wiped clean. Forgiven of his own large debt, the man went out and promptly encountered a friend who owed him a much smaller sum. He grabbed his friend by the throat and demanded, "Pay me every cent you owe me, or else I will have you thrown into prison." It didn't matter that he had just been forgiven of a debt 64,000 times greater than what his friend owed him. He was totally unwilling to forgive. Jesus rebuked this sort of attitude and taught that those who have been shown compassion need to show it to others.

Our apathy does not come from lack of knowledge as to what we should do, nor is it that we resist doing what we know we should. It's just that we never quite get around to doing those things we know are right and expected of us. We have often heard that the road to hell is paved with good intentions. Well, for some Christians, so is the road to heaven. George Sweeting has said that "The road marked *Tomorrow* leads to the town called *Never*."

No amount of intelligence, promotion or finances will ever make up for an apathetic church. Where apathy prevails, well-meaning men become disillusioned and misdirected; programs become ends in themselves and prove empty; and money is wasted. Apathy unchecked or uncorrected marks the beginning of the end for any movement.

APATHY LEADS TO LACK OF APPRECIATION FOR GOD'S PAST BLESSINGS

Israel was constantly reminded by the prophets to rehearse before each succeeding generation the rich blessings of God upon His people. This gave rise to a reoccurring faith in God to continue His work among His children. The church is plagued by a loss of memory. When we forget what God has done, we cease to thank Him for

His past blessings and we lose sight of our future possibilities. Without a sense of history we can have no assurance of a future.

God has moved mightily in the Church of God. Our early days were marked by regular supernatural occurrences which produced growth in the face of seemingly insurmountable circumstances. We can ill afford to forget those blessings and pass them off as being part of an era which was not as enlightened or as educated as ours.

The psalmist reminds us that God "established a testimony in Jacob, and appointed a law in Israel, which he commanded our fathers, that they should make them known to their children: That the generation to come might know them, even the children which should be born; who should arise and declare them to their children: That they might set their hope in God, and not forget the works of God, but keep his commandments" (Psalm 78:5-7).

More than 22 years of my life have been spent in ministry to young people. I have been absolutely absorbed with the burning desire to see this new generation embrace, uphold and defend those tenets of faith which led our early church members to make such incalculable commitments and sacrifices. I have also invested a great deal of myself in trying to establish a glowing hope for the future of our church in the hearts of those youth. I am saddened to say, however, that many of this generation have little knowledge of the unfailing commitment of that generation of early believers. They have only a passing acquaintance with those miracles of divine intervention that paved the way for this modern-day Pentecostal awakening. It is equally sad that these same young people have so little hope for the future.

Can't we see it? It is an undeniable scriptural principle. If we don't share with our young people the blessings of the past, they will have no basis for future hopes. We can't separate our future from our past. If we forget the past, we forfeit our right to God's future promises. Apathy steals our past and robs us of hope.

APATHY LEADS TO PRESUMPTION

Dr. Horace Ward has defined *presumption* as one part good intentions and one part arrogance. The danger of presumption is a false conclusion that just because God has been with us, He always will be.

Judah made the sad mistake of presumption. For centuries the prophets had foretold that out of Judah would come the Messiah, King of the Jews. The people of Judah felt they had such favor with God it didn't really matter how they lived. Because of this presumption, they missed out on the greatest event of history. They didn't even recognize the Messiah when He came. Make no mistake about it, God will bring judgment on any people who presume on His grace and mercy.

If we listen carefully to those Christian leaders who have recently fallen into sin, we will hear the same story that has been repeated for centuries by those who failed God. It goes something like this: "I never intended to fail God and bring disgrace on the body of Christ. I just took too much for granted. I felt because I had been so committed to the work of God and because I had been so successful, God would not allow me to go beyond that point of immediate restoration."

Several years ago I talked with a fellow who had served as the right-hand man of an evangelist who had experienced great results in his evangelistic crusades. Later in life, however, this man reportedly became addicted to alcohol and eventually lost his ministry because of public drunkenness.

I asked the fellow who had worked closely with him, "Did you know the man was drinking when you worked with him?" He implied that he did but that the evangelist maintained such "close contact with God" that his drunkenness never affected his evangelistic results.

When asked to explain what he meant, the man said, "Well, when he got drunk, he would spend several days praying and fasting for forgiveness; and when he emerged, he would go straight into another evangelistic crusade and God would use him mightily. When the crusade was over, he would go out and get drunk to celebrate."

Unfortunately, this poor man presumed on the grace of God. Sure, God forgave him when he prayed. But there came a point where God said, "Enough. You can't continue violating My Word without coming under My judgment." The judgment of God seems to go a little deeper each time. God's initial judgment is but prelude to the judgment He will pour out if His call for repentance goes unheeded. This man's fall was great, and many people were disillusioned and hurt.

William Martin, Rice University sociologist, said of a minister who had recently fallen into sin: "I think what happens to this kind of person is that he begins to think, 'I couldn't have come this far if not for God.' Then he begins to say, 'Well, if I have this idea to build a Bible college or a mission, it must have come from God.' Next he starts to say, 'God told me this. God told me that.' And the next step from there is that he says, 'I think what God meant to say was...!'"(*People Weekly*, March 7, 1988, p. 37).

The psalmist prayed, "Keep back thy servant also from presumptuous sins; let them not have dominion over me: then shall I be upright, and I shall be innocent from the great transgression" (Psalm 19:13).

Apathy leads to presumptuous sins.

APATHY LEADS TO LACK OF COMMITMENT

Jesus taught that He alone could meet the needs of men. He was confident no one else could give what He was capable of giving. He promised a life of profound usefulness and satisfaction, and He promised it to anyone who would believe, regardless of personal background or limitations. He saw the overwhelming needs of man and was filled with the consciousness that He alone could offer genuine peace and full meaning to life. This is why He gave Himself so totally to the mission He was sent to fulfill. He completely emptied Himself to see that His job on earth was complete, and not one time did He cling to His personal prerogative as the Son of God.

The powerful reality that the church is to carry on the work of Christ on earth should constantly give us a sense of commitment unparalleled by any other cause. No

Chief Obstacle to Renewal

"I suppose one of
the most difficult
things for me to
understand is how
some people give
such high-rate at-
tention to such
low-rate causes...."

The **Pain** and the **Glory**

man can be part of the body of Christ and not be touched by the plight of human need. To be rightly related to God through Christ is to have a compassionate feeling toward all men, regardless of their color or ethnic origin. In our land with its polyglot population, we need to be sure we have a religious life that will stand the test of such a definition.

One of the most important questions we face in life is to what cause will we commit ourselves. It is an important question because life itself is at stake. To choose less than the best as our object of loyalty is to condemn ourselves to a lifetime of mediocrity. The great need of every life is a sense of loyalty which allows one to centralize energies and provide a sense of mission. The happiest and most fulfilled people on earth are those who feel a sense of divine purpose that God does indeed have something to do with what they are doing in life. On the other hand, the most unfulfilled people on earth are those who waste their lives on nothingness because they have never found any cause big enough to grip their lives and to give purpose to their activity.

I suppose one of the most difficult things for me to understand is how some people give such high-rate attention to such low-rate causes, while there are those who are supposedly committed to noble causes and give them so little attention.

As a teenager I met "the goat man," who traveled across America with a wagon--goats in the wagon and goats walking behind the wagon. I asked him why he had chosen this as his lot in life and he said, "Because I love goats." Now I have nothing in particular against goats, but

I don't think they are worthy of such total commitment. I remember thinking how strange it was that this fellow was willing to sacrifice his comfort and well-being for the sake of his goat herd while some Christians I knew were not willing to sacrifice for the greatest cause on earth—the salvation of souls.

The cause of Christ is indeed the greatest cause on earth, and He demands the undying loyalty of all who follow Him. The salvation of the world cost God more and requires more from men than any movement in history. Why then is there such a calculated indifference on the part of some churches to the world's needs? Why have so many Christians ceased to tell the story with great fervency? Could it be that we have allowed ritual and formality to crowd out the spontaneous and natural testimony that we knew as a newly born child of God?

To live in a world of unsaved people and not try to win them is a terrible, horrible thing. To live in a world of guilt, trouble and pain, knowing that we have the cure and not sharing it, is a flagrant violation of God's grace. We must always be sensitive to finding the Lord's way of leading lost souls out of spiritual darkness into the eternal joy of serving Jesus Christ.

Some Christians give a polite nod to commitment but are never willing to get involved in the Lord's work. When William Carey, the great missionary, refuted the arguments of those who insisted that missionary endeavors were simply too difficult, he reminded them that, since the invention of the compass, even heathen navigators could sail the great South Sea as easily as they could the Mediterranean. He reminded fellow ministers, "It only requires that we should have as much love to the souls of our fellow creatures...as they have from the profits arising from a few *otter-skins*." Once men become committed to the Lord they quickly put their faith into action. The straight road to renewal is the road of obedience.

APATHY LEADS TO HARDNESS OF HEART

The problem with apathy is that we can't set the limits as to how far astray from established principles of human concern it will lead us. I recently heard a Jewish man who lived in Europe during World War II say of Hitler's atrocities, "When he first started persecuting those persons who were non-white, I said, 'There's no need to get involved.' Then he began persecuting the educated; then the professionals; then Catholics; then the wealthy. Each time I would say, 'There's no need to get involved.' By the time he got around to the Jews there was no one left to get involved."

Apathy is the prelude to hardness of the heart. It causes people to close their eyes to the troubles and woes of others, to become first insensitive, then noncaring and finally hardened. Nothing is more dangerous than when God turns a person over to a hard heart. The atrocities of Pharaoh against the children of Israel were because the "Lord hardened Pharaoh's heart" (Exodus 7:13).

That the judgment of God has come upon the church is indisputable. We have watched ministry empires rise, and we have watched them fall. We have seen men soar to fame and power, and we have watched them topple in shame and disgrace. It appears certain that God, although long-suffering and tolerant with His church, will not allow His commandments to be forever disregarded and His grace to be used as a license to fulfill one's own goals and ambitions. God will bring all of man's work under divine judgment. The question then is not "Have I been successful?" or "Have I maintained an acceptable image?" The only question that matters when one's life and work are brought under divine scrutiny is this: "Have I been faithful to Him who has called me out of darkness into His marvelous light?"

Apathy cannot live where there is a spiritual hunger for righteousness, a longing for a deeper and richer fellowship with Jesus Christ, and an insatiable desire for fellowship with God. Isaiah says,

> *And if thou draw out thy soul to the hungry, and satisfy the afflicted soul; then shall thy light rise in obscurity, and thy darkness be as the noon day: And the Lord shall guide thee continually, and satisfy thy soul in draught, and make fat thy bones: and thou shalt be like a watered garden, and like a spring of water, whose waters fail not. And they shat shall be of these shall build the old waste places: thou shalt raise up the foundations of many generations; and thou shalt be called, The repairer of the breach, The restorer of paths to dwell in* (Isaiah 58:10-12).

The Church of God has historically been characterized by a passion for obeying God, regardless of the cost. The secret of our extraordinary fellowship has always been our shared passions. As a movement we have been pressed by a passion for righteousness, for revival and for souls. Do we still share those same passions, regardless of the size or location of our church?

The church is portrayed in Revelation as wrapped in a deep sleep, with the Lord trying to arouse her. He appeals, "Behold, I stand at the door, and knock: if any man hear my voice, and open the door, I will come in to him, and will sup with him, and he with me" (Revelation 3:20).

A sleeping church is of no value to God. An apathetic people cannot save an apathetic world. A jaded church cannot stir people to higher purpose. A man or woman who has lost the glory and the glow cannot impart these jewels to others.

As long as there is a Cross at the center of our faith, we can never be apathetic.

———————————

Principles
of
Renewal

1
Being Thankful for Past Blessings

2
Avoiding Presumption

3
Remembering Our Commitment

4
Remaining Sensitive to the Holy
Spirit

"Genuine spiritual renewal --personal or corporate--can never take place until minds and attitudes are changed."

3

OUR MINDS SEEM CON- FUSED

Our generation has seen more scientific and technological advancements than any other. We have not been content to tolerate the limitations and discomforts of our ancestors. Yet, while we are blazing new trails through the solar system, knocking on the doors of neighboring planets, probing deeply into the psyche of man and seeking truth in every field of study, we seem content to stand still where spiritual matters are concerned. Now is the time for us to come face-to-face with the realities of the spiritual victories God has promised us in His Word. Every facet of man—spirit, body and mind—is needed if we are to receive the fullness of God's spiritual promises. It is especially important that we open our minds to the possibilities of everything God has planned for us.

Genuine spiritual renewal—personal or corporate—can never take place until minds and attitudes are changed. In Ephesians Paul encourages, "Be renewed in the spirit of your mind" (Ephesians 4:23). The *Goodspeed* translation says, "You must adopt a new attitude of mind."

Far too many Christians are so wedded to the past that they can only think in terms of what God has done rather than what He wishes to do presently and in the future. George Mallone tells of a story related by Canadian journalist Peter Newman.

Newman was covering his first news event in the maritime provinces and was trying to make small talk with one of the farmers. He inquired, "Have you lived here all of your life?" The farmer thought for a moment and replied, "No, not yet."

Newman was expecting an answer that reflected the man's past, but the answer he received gave indication of a man looking toward the future. This is the way Christians should describe their experience with the Lord. A new attitude of mind should cause us to respond, "Thank God for the mysteries of His Word He has already uncovered for me. But I am equally excited about what He plans to reveal to me." A renewed mind keeps the heart open.

Mark Twain once told a friend whom he thought was going stale, "Take your mind out and jump up and down on it; it's getting all caked up." Sometimes we need to jump up and down on our traditional concepts to see whether or not they have become set in concrete and steel. We need to discover whether these concepts are really ours or rather something we have accepted from others without ever having thought them through for ourselves. People who get so wrapped up in past traditions that they cannot be sensitive to what the Holy Spirit is wanting to accomplish today are desperately in need of renewal.

The Apostle Paul prayed, "That the God of our Lord Jesus Christ, the Father of glory, may give unto you the spirit of wisdom and revelation in the knowledge of him: The eyes of your understanding being enlightened; that ye may know what is the hope of his calling" (Ephesians 1:17, 18). It is interesting to note that Paul did not pray for a revival of supernatural manifestations. He prayed that believers may have fuller knowledge of God and of what God desires to do through them. It is only through a fuller knowledge of God, imparted by the Holy Spirit, that God's people can move in harmony with His Holy Spirit. It is through knowledge of God that our beliefs in God are formed.

There is an inseparable connection between the intellect and the obedience of man to the call of God. We accept first with our minds and then we put the rest of our faculties behind what we accept conceptually to be right. God has promised to enlighten "the eyes of our heart." It is God who gives us insight. It ought then to be the prayer of every believer, "Open Thou mine eyes, that I may see wondrous things of Thy law."

The **Pain** and the **Glory**

Dale Oldham in some lecture notes on the New Testament wrote about the response of Nicodemus to Christ's teachings about the New Birth, "It was outside his groove: rote, rut, rot, the three terrible R's of traditionalism." Nicodemus was so involved in platitudes and traditionalism that his mind could not grasp a fact outside the beaten path of his habitual thinking. What a tragedy it is for a Christian to become so locked into routine thinking that God cannot break through with new revelations of His goodness and promises.

Rote means "routine, or repetition carried out mechanically or unthinkingly." I can't help but think of the countless Christians who say prayers which have lost their meaning or sing the words to old hymns with passive expressions or perform religious deeds with obvious triteness. There is no sense of purpose or goal in anything they do. Their one aim is to avoid doing anything that may keep them out of heaven when life on earth has ended. They simply toil along the Christian pathway.

The second of the three terrible R's of traditionalism is *rut*. Someone has defined a rut as a grave with both ends knocked out. Even in a day such as ours, when God is pouring out His Spirit in such a fantastic manner, thousands of Christians still live from one incident to another, looking forward only to one hope—an escape from what they call the "burdens of life." How can people live in such measly existence when God has promised us limitless dimensions of the spiritual life?

God help us to stay out of spiritual ruts. We need to blaze new trails into the secrets of Jesus' way of life. We need to make vivid to this world the triumphant Christ who, through His death, freed men from death and bondage and who opened to us untold possibilities for spiritual adventure by His resurrection. Most of the sadness and drudgery of this world would disappear if we really took Jesus at His Word and began to transform the little we have into the spiritual values of life.

The inevitable end of rote and rut is *rot*. When the spring ceases to flow, it stagnates. The moment you and I cease to grow spiritually we begin to die. There is no standing still. Spiritual death is a tragic thing which need not happen.

Admittedly, it is not easy to live a spiritual life in earthly surroundings. The things of earth are so close we become more interested in what we see with the natural eye than in what we may see through the eyes of our spirit.

William Blake sums it up in this little poem:

This life's dim window of the soul
Distort the heavens from pole to pole
And lead you to believe a lie
When you see with, not through the eye.

A renewal of concepts—how we think—begins when God's Spirit illuminates our mind and our inner spirit and our eyes are opened to what God wants to do in this world through His church. The gift of spiritual vision is one of the surest proofs of the presence of God within us. Once we know what God wants to do, it is then up to us whether we will cooperate. God's work will be done. He will have a people. He will find individuals or some group who will be sensitive to the moving of His Holy

The **Pain** and the **Glory**

Spirit on earth. Conceptual renewal will bring about a new openness to what God desires to do among His people.

RENEWAL OF CONCEPTS BROADENS OUR FAITH IN GOD TO ACT

Within recent decades we have seen a growing number of denominations become open to the gifts of the Spirit. Prayer for the sick is now being offered in many non-Pentecostal churches, and many individuals in main-line denominations are testifying to having been baptized with the Holy Spirit. Prophecies are now being uttered in some congregations that a few years ago would have dismissed such possibilities as totally impossible and would have dismissed those giving the prophecies as well. It is evident God is willing to move in the midst of a yielded people today with the same power and authority with which He has moved in the past.

The Pentecostal Movement has always been characterized by simple faith in God to do what He says. If God said it, that was proof positive it would be done. Embracing a "full gospel" message, we have held forth on such things as divine healing, divine intervention in the daily affairs of men, the baptism of the Holy Spirit with the evidence of speaking in tongues as the Spirit gives utterance, and in the future hope of eschatological events. Unfortunately, there seems to have been an erosion of some of these beliefs.

Some of the so-called "faith healers" and "preachers of prosperity" and the far-out prophecy preachers have

"Regardless of what man says or does...it does not change God's Holy Word. Anything God has said can be counted on."

caused some Pentecostals to back away from those things which we have for years believed were part of God's plan for us. If we think for one moment that false teaching and egocentric preaching influence God to curtail His activity among a yielded and open-minded people, we need to rethink our theology. Regardless of what man says or does, or regardless of how some people may misuse the Word and the gifts God gave them, it does not change God's Holy Word. Anything God has said can be counted on.

The people of God must have faith in God. That unfailing faith in God is what keeps God's people from a dependency on the arm of flesh. Faith keeps a clear focus on the promises and the provisions of God. Faith keeps us from being restricted by the obvious and from being enslaved by circumstances. Those who trust in anything but God will suffer great loss when the arm of flesh is removed or when worldly foundations are shaken. On the other hand, "They that trust in the Lord shall be as mount Zion, which cannot be removed, but abideth for ever" (Psalm 125:1).

RENEWAL OF CONCEPTS OPENS US TO GOD'S SOVEREIGN GRACE

It's time we realize we cannot tell God when and where He can or cannot move. The Holy Spirit is strangely democratic. He works where some people don't quite think He should. God has a unique way of sometimes bypassing the normal structure and contradicting the traditional concepts as to how He is to move among mankind. God's way always cuts across the counsel of the world and often baffles His own people, but He will not be captive to our traditionalism. The great clash Jesus had with religious leaders of His time centered around His concern for the welfare of people rather than for structure.

Several years ago I was invited to preach an interdenominational community crusade. One of the host pastors reminded me many people would be hearing a Pentecostal preacher for the first time and that I need not be alarmed if they were not as responsive as my accustomed audience. They were more responsive. One night I felt especially impressed of the Lord to pray for the sick. I quoted Hebrews 13:8—"Jesus Christ the same yesterday, and to day, and for ever." Then I asked for those who needed healing to stand, encouraging those seated around them to lay hands on them while we prayed.

Suddenly, I heard a shout of praise from the back of the auditorium. I watched as a lady made her way down the aisle, jumping up and down as she came. Reaching the edge of the platform, she looked up at me and asked, "Father, can you tell me what's happening?" She was obviously Catholic, not accustomed to anything like this.

"Well, first of all, I'm not a Catholic priest. Second, why don't you tell me what's happening? You're the one doing all the shouting and jumping."

"I've been deaf in one ear for more than seven years, and I never knew God could still heal. When you quoted that scripture, I said to my friend who came with me tonight, he looks like an honest man. If he says it, I guess I believe it. Someone laid hands on me, and all of a sudden

I could hear out of my deaf ear. Next thing I knew I was down here."

I explained that God had healed her. I also invited her to attend the local Church of God where I would be preaching on Sunday. She came, and God filled her with the Holy Spirit.

I understand that some of the members were upset because God had healed a Roman Catholic and filled her with the Holy Spirit on her first visit. It really didn't seem fair at all because some of them had been seeking the Holy Spirit for years and had not been filled. Perhaps it is time we understand God will heal whomsoever He pleases. His Holy Spirit is available to all who are redeemed and open to the deeper spiritual life.

Many in the New Testament church wanted to make the church Jewish. They did not believe one could be a Christian without first buying into all the form and ritual of Judaism. It took a vision and the voice of God to make Peter willing to accept the call of the Roman centurion Cornelius and share the gospel with him. Peter had to go through a complete transformation in order to say, "I perceive that God is no respecter of persons." Even after that he was called before the Jerusalem Council to vindicate his ministry to the Gentiles. Perhaps if we were to develop the same prayer habits as Peter and Cornelius we too would have enlarged visions of God's openness to all who believe.

RENEWAL OF CONCEPTS DEEPENS OUR DEPENDENCY ON THE HOLY SPIRIT

"We seem to think that if we put our best foot forward we can win this world to Christ. We can no more do that than a spider's web can entangle a Titan missile."

The **Pain** and the **Glory**

Most everything we do is explained in terms of human effort. When we work hard, things seem to happen. When we don't work hard, things seem not to happen. Whatever happened to our belief in the supernatural, our belief that all we have to do is be obedient and God will bring His Word to pass?

We are more image-oriented today than we are concept-oriented. We seem more concerned with acceptance than with accuracy. The idea that success breeds success leads us to strive for immediate results more than for long-lasting effects. We seem to think that if we put our best foot forward we can win this world to Christ. We can no more do that than a spider's web can entangle a Titan missile. God's work must be done God's way. Our responsibility is to get our hearts and minds in tune with what He wants to do.

True spiritual renewal will never take place as long as we believe we can pull it off ourselves. It is when we reach the place where we have no more solutions that God steps in. If we are entirely successful within ourselves, there is a tendency to rely on the arm of the flesh. We lose a sense of awe at the presence of God and begin to applaud our own accomplishments.

We say we will have renewal when all conditions are conducive. Historically, conditions are ripe for renewal when the circumstances are all wrong, when all hope seems lost, when declension and decay rule the day, when we have lost faith in the arm of flesh, and nothing but renewal will put things right again. We say, "Where there is life, there is hope." God says, "Where there is death, life can spring forth again. I will breathe upon your dead bones, and they will live again."

Renewal is not something we do. All of the promotions and programs in the world cannot bring about genuine spiritual renewal. Only God brings renewal. Paul says, "Not by works of righteousness which we have done, but according to his mercy he saved us, by the washing of regeneration, and renewing of the Holy Ghost" (Titus 3:5). Our responsibility is to prepare our hearts and minds to receive this kind of renewal.

RENEWAL OF CONCEPTS STRESSES THE REVOLUTIONARY ELEMENTS OF THE GOSPEL

Christianity has always been revolutionary in its message. It storms the enemy's territory, overturning all that is ungodly and uprooting evil wherever it is found. When Christian zeal or fervor becomes anything less than revolutionary, it ceases to capture the imagination and attention of the world. It is time for the Christian church once again to flex its spiritual and mental muscles and shock people out of stagnant indifference into deep conviction of the need of God. Our trouble does not lie in a powerless gospel but in believers who are not living convincing lives.

From the beginning men have been drawn to Jesus Christ by His love and His power. The hungry were fed, sick people were made well, dead men were raised to new life. If we are to realize the purpose for which God has

61

allowed us to live in this special period of human history, we must follow in His steps. The church is meant to be the channel and organism by which that spiritual power is made available today. The church has often attempted to offer a substitute for spiritual power, but no one is fooled. When we reach out with our gimmicks, this world doesn't even blink an eye. She goes right on sleeping the sleep of death.

Far too many Christian leaders are satisfied to be managers for the *status quo*. My prayer is "God make us discontent with the *status quo* so that we will endeavor to release Your blessed power upon the sick and fearful and unreached and bewildered and seeking folk of our day. Help us gain a militant faith which will not permit satisfaction in the midst of Your grace and power while a dying world needs to hear the message You have committed to us."

RENEWAL OF CONCEPTS HEIGHTENS THE FOCUS OF OUR MISSION

Apart from the fulfillment of its supreme mission to preach the gospel to every creature and to pray for the kingdom of God to be on earth as it is in heaven, the church has no reason to exist. Mission is to the church what fire is to burning. Take away the fire—there is no burning. Take away the mission—there is no church.

In his book *The All-Sufficient Christ* (1963, pp. 111,112), William Barclay shares an account of a man in India who came to a pastor pleading to be allowed to become a member of the church. The pastor knew this man had no previous connection with the church and that he had not received any previous instruction about church membership, at least not from him. Naturally the pastor wanted to be certain the man knew what he was doing. "Tell me," he said, "why you are so anxious to become a member of the church."

The man replied, "By chance there came into my hands a copy of Luke's Gospel. I read it and I thought that I had never heard of anyone so wise and wonderful as Jesus, and I wished to take him as my Master and my Lord. But at that stage I thought that it was simply a matter between him and me and no one else. Then by chance I got a copy of the book of the Acts. Here was a difference. Luke was all about what Jesus said and did. But at the end of Luke, Jesus ascends to his Father, and Acts begins with the same story. In The Acts, Jesus is no more on earth in the flesh. The Acts is not so much about what Jesus said and did as it is about what Peter and Paul said and did, and above all, about what the church said and did. So," said the man, "I felt I must become a member of that church which carries on the life of Christ."

Why is it the church today seems sometimes to be in great contrast to the New Testament church? For one thing, the New Testament church never lost sight of its purpose. The people knew why they were on earth and not in heaven. They believed Jesus left them here to do a work, and they were actively in pursuit of that mission. Essential to that mission was close communion with Christ through the Holy Spirit.

Can we so yield ourselves to the Holy Spirit that He

can fill us with power to take this world for Jesus Christ?

The Holy Spirit is not dead. He can still speak, and He *is* speaking to those who are open to hear what He has to say. The Holy Spirit works in us to stir up our "pure minds" to remember His Word and His work. To resist the strivings of the Holy Spirit, or even to be indifferent to them, is a tragic and deadly sin.

———————————

PRINCIPLES
OF
RENEWAL

1
Expanded Faith

2
God's Sovereign Grace

3
Dependance on the Holy Spirit

4
A Revolutionary Gospel

5
Focus on Mission

"We cannot expect to have a vibrant relationship with God for nothing. A price must be paid."

4

We Are Each Responsible

The frantic pace of our 20th-century lifestyles often causes Christians to shift attention and energy from those things that are central to those things that are peripheral in nature. Our busyness often causes us to lose sight of our true priorities. Whether life is a routine or a romance depends on where we place our priorities. The dietitian more concerned about pots and pans than the nutrition of the children she feeds has lost sight of priorities. The politician more concerned about votes than serving his constituency has lost sight of priorities. The airline pilot more concerned about peanuts and soda pop in the passengers' cabins than in safety has lost sight of priorities. The Christian more concerned with temporal matters than eternal values of the Word has lost sight of priorities.

The **Pain** and the **Glory**

Not many people ever start out to lose a vibrant relationship with God. They just drift into it. When a pilot takes off from Los Angeles for New York, he immediately sets his course. If he does not periodically adjust his course, he will miss New York City by hundreds of miles. Several variables enter into the flight picture. Wind velocity and direction may change. Atmospheric conditions or changes in the weight of the aircraft because of fuel usage may alter the course. The important thing is that a skilled pilot knows that when changes occur, he must adjust his course.

Life itself does not remain constant. We are often faced with changes that upset the normalcy of routines and throw good intentions out of kilter. Things happen, sometimes on purpose and sometimes accidentally, which put our well-meaning plans off course. The ups and downs of life keep us struggling for balance. We have to push forward, look upward, gain new insights, make new commitments, discipline ourselves to those principles which promote growth and understanding. Static existence is sure death.

The path to spiritual death is so natural and easy we scarcely realize it is happening. It begins when we deliberately suppress truth or refuse to receive it. We know we ought to pray and read God's Word more than we do, but we just never seem to find time. Convicted every time we hear a message on personal devotions, we vow to change—but we don't. Spiritual renewal never comes cheaply. We cannot expect to have a vibrant relationship with God for nothing. A price must be paid.

Many Christians have never developed an inner

capacity for a spiritual relationship with God. They get uncomfortable when God gets close. But with God there is no halfway ground. Neutrality is just not possible when it comes to Christian living. Jesus' way of life presents stern alternatives. Those who are not with Him are against Him. Those who don't gather scatter abroad. Those who don't love Him hate Him.

Few of us ever suspect those spiritual realities denied because we won't pay the price. Like weary travelers too tired to climb the peak from which to view the real beauty, we drop by the mall and view colorful posters in the travel center.

To those who have known the joy of personal communion with God, however, no substitute will suffice. Perfunctory service and half-hearted worship serve only to send sharp messages to the heart—something is wrong. To ignore that message leads to hypocrisy, going through the motions with full knowledge that something is lacking in personal relationship with God.

No account of personal renewal is more poignant than that of Jacob (Genesis 35), a man who got out of step with God and reaped a harvest of shame and disgrace. However, Jacob realized God was available and ready to restore him to all the joys he had known. Jacob left God: God did not leave Jacob. Therefore, the act of returning was totally in Jacob's prerogative. He made the right choice. Perhaps a retracing of Jacob's steps to personal renewal will assist us in our own journey.

JACOB REACHED A PLACE OF PERSONAL DESPERATION

The **Pain** and the **Glory**

Sad to say, many people never bother with God as long as everything goes well. Sometimes God has to allow us to reach a place of absolute desperation before we confess our need for Him. Such was the case with Jacob.

Jacob was blessed of God. He was heir to all the promises and blessings of his grandfather Abraham. He had a personal encounter with God in which God promised, "Behold, I am with thee, and will keep thee in all places whither thou goest, and will bring thee again into this land; for I will not leave thee, until I have done that which I have spoken to thee of" (Genesis 28:15).

Jacob had been given a promise and a dream for the future. However, it was a dream that soon turned sour. He forgot the promises he had made God, soon abandoned the place of blessing, and was without an altar in his house. He gained an evil name among the nations, so much so that he lamented to his sons, "Ye have troubled me to make me to stink among the inhabitants of the land" (Genesis 34:30).

Imagine that! A man who was so blessed of God, a man who was a direct descendant of Abraham, a man who was chosen of God—a stink in the land! The steps that lead away from personal relationship with God rarely stop before ending in personal or family tragedy.

Jacob woke one morning to say, "This is not the way I intended things to turn out. Something has gone wrong with the dream. My daughter has become involved with the wrong crowd, and now she has been raped. My sons have been deceitful and have resorted to murder. I have abandoned my birthright and have failed to keep my promises to God. My family and I are not the heirs of promise. We have become a foul odor throughout the

"Sad to say, many people never bother with God so long as everything goes well."

land. Oh God, something must change."

When Jacob reached that place of absolute desperation, he decided to do something about his relationship
with God. It is not necessary to wait that long before
making a move back to God. Perhaps, though, each of us
must in our own way sense a feeling of helplessness.
Perhaps we too must experience a feeling of desperation.
That may well be God's way of saying, "I am still here and
I am still available to help. You don't have to go it alone."

JACOB HEARD THE VOICE OF GOD

The Bible says, "And God said unto Jacob, Arise,
go up to Bethel" (Genesis 35:1).

Always among us are those who snub the idea of
anyone hearing the voice of God. Such an experience is
usually considered outdated, or it is assigned to the weird,
super religious or mentally troubled. God has not stopped
speaking. Maybe we have just quit listening.

God does not necessarily have to jolt us with a
booming voice from the mountain, or a burning bush
experience, or handwriting on the wall to communicate.
Sometimes He whispers in a still, small inner voice, which
prompts us to take some action. Think for a moment. Do
you remember the last time God prompted you to some
positive action? It may have been through a sermon, a
song, a conversation with a friend, or it may have been
during a time of quiet meditation; but at the moment you
felt God was trying to break through with a message. Go
back and recall those moments. Remember what God was

saying. That may turn out to be the beginning of your own personal renewal.

We must never forget how much God cares for the smallest details of our lives. Before we were conceived in our mother's womb, God knew us (Psalm 139:13-16). Jesus said the very hairs of our head are numbered (Matthew 10:30). We do matter to God, and He does not easily leave us to our own folly. He will whisper to us or shout at us. He may gently nudge us or shake us, but He *will* get our attention.

JACOB PUT AWAY HINDRANCES

Jacob knew some things had to be eliminated from his life if he were to be restored to special communion with God. He took charge of the situation and removed those things which hindered spiritual progress: "Then Jacob said unto his household, and to all that were with him, Put away the strange gods that are among you, and be clean, and change your garments" (Genesis 35:2).

There are many hindrances to spiritual life. Anything that competes with quality time with God—with prayer, Bible study or worship—can be a hindrance. Something does not necessarily have to be bad to compete with spiritual life. In fact, most competition with spiritual life comes from wholesome, well-meaning and sometimes necessary activities. Take recreational activities, for example. God wants us to spend time in activities which keep the body healthy. Yet, when recreation becomes more important than spiritual growth, when recreation takes more time than we devote to spiritual well-being, it becomes a hindrance with which to deal.

Spiritual hindrances come in all forms and descriptions. I have a friend who no longer watches television. It's not that he feels there is anything inherently wrong with TV. For him it became such a hindrance to his prayer and devotional life that he has chosen to eliminate TV viewing. Some may scorn him as fanatical, but I admire a man who will so prioritize his life that God has top billing.

Jacob knew he could never make it right with God unless he was willing to make it right with his brother whom he had wronged. When he met Esau he declared, "I have seen thy face, as though I had seen the face of God" (Genesis 33:10). Until we are willing to make restitution and to be reconciled with those whom we have wronged, there is no hope of personal renewal. We must see our offended brother or sister as we see God. There is immense need for renewal of relationships in the church, both vertically toward God and horizontally toward our brothers and sisters.

Sin in any form or fashion blocks spiritual progress. Sin is like a wall. It keeps us from God and stops the flow of God's blessings to us. Sin will not go away on its own. It never has and never will. Sin is like a malignant cancer. It grows until it is removed. The passing of time may ease the conscience, but it will not remove sin. There is only one way to get rid of sin--through confession, repentance and faith in the blood of Jesus Christ.

Whatever thought, activity or attitude that keeps you from reaching that place of sweet communion with

God is a hindrance and should be eliminated. Of course, it may be painful and may require a radical change in your life, but the benefits far surpass any of earth's alluring alternatives.

The consequence is broken fellowship with God.

JACOB RETURNED TO THE PLACE WHERE HE HAD ENCOUNTERED GOD

Renewal almost always involves returning (if not physically, then in mind and spirit) to those places where life commitments were made and where special encounters with God were noted. For Jacob, it was a return to Bethel. It was here where God met him in the day of distress and promised to be with him wherever he went. It was at Bethel where Jacob had made some promises to God, promises that had long been forgotten. It was at Bethel where Jacob had the Abrahamic Covenant confirmed to him, where the spiritual contents of faith were actualized. Jacob went back to Bethel to recapture the vision and to reaffirm his commitment to God.

If your keen zest for spiritual life is gone, for God's sake, get it back. How? Like Jacob, go back where you last encountered God. Every Christian has his or her Bethel. God will meet you at the precise point where you had your last meaningful encounter with Him. Maybe He showed you some sin in your life that you never gave up. Maybe He asked you to do something and you turned away because you thought it was too difficult. Maybe He pointed out the need for some changes in your life which

The **Pain** and the **Glory**

you never got around to making. Wherever it was, He is still there. Go back to that moment and He will meet you. Old passages of Scripture will take on new meaning. New light will dawn. New hope will spring from the ashes of lost dreams.

JACOB BUILT AN ALTAR

The first thing Jacob did when he arrived at Bethel was to build an altar, which he called El-beth-el (Genesis 35:7). That is significant. When he was first at this place, he had a vision of a ladder which stretched from earth to heaven. He was so impressed that he called the place "Bethel," or "The house of God." Now he was more concerned about the God of the place than he was the place, so he called it El-Bethel, or "The God of the house of God."

The great need of our time is for men and women who have a mind for God. This is even more important than having men and women who have a mind for ministry. People who have a mind for God will find a ministry. People who have a mind for ministry don't always find God.

People who have a mind for God pray. To them prayer is more than a periodic emphasis or a passing fad. It is a lifestyle. It is a life line. It is as vital to their spiritual health as food and water to their physical well-being. E. M. Bounds was such a man. He left the security of a pastorate to arouse others to the urgent need for prayer. He wrote, "Praying is spiritual work; and human nature does

76

"God will meet you at the precise point where you had your last meaning- ful encounter with Him."

not like taxing, spiritual work. Human nature wants to sail to heaven under a favoring breeze, a full, smooth sea....So we come to one of the crying evils of these times, maybe of all times—little or no praying. Of these two evils, perhaps little praying is worse than no praying. Little praying is a kind of make-believe, a salvo for the conscience, a farce and a delusion" (*Power Through Prayer,* 1986, p. 36).

A recommitment to prayer ushers in a renewed commitment to a personal devotion to the Word. Unfaithfulness to prayer and the Word leads us into the realm of worldly pursuits where there is no fellowship with God. God and His Word must become the absorbing and irresistible center of our lives.

JACOB RENEWED HIS COVENANTS

God is a covenant-honoring God. He is faithful to the covenants He has made with man. The psalmist says, "He hath remembered his covenant forever, the word which he commanded to a thousand generations" (Psalm 105:8). God also requires that man be faithful to his covenants with God. In Ecclesiastes 5:4 we read, "When thou vowest a vow unto God, defer not to pay it; for he hath no pleasure in fools: pay that which thou hast vowed."

The idea of covenant originated with God. According to Van A. Harvey, "A covenant is a relationship between two parties...in which each party voluntarily agrees to certain conditions of the relationship and gives his word to uphold it" (*A Handbook of Theological Terms,*

1979, p. 60). A covenant differs from a contract or an agreement in that it is permanent and irrevocable. God has persisted in keeping His covenants with us although we have fallen woefully short in keeping ours. However, God extends to us a call to renew our covenants with Him.

Any move toward renewal will involve a recalling and a recommitment to the covenants we have made with God. Among the first of those covenants was our commitment to live for God regardless of the sacrifices or the circumstances. Although it is not required of the Christian to continue "laying again the foundation of repentance" (Hebrews 6:1), it is required that we return often to those promises of life commitment when God for Christ's sake forgave us of sin. Renewal often involves bitter tears of repentance and remorse. Renewal always involves recommitment to our covenants with God.

Besides those covenants we have made with God, the two other most sacred covenants are marriage covenants and those we have made with the church. Unfortunately, there has been a lapse in both areas. Marriage covenants are sacred and cannot be violated without serious moral and spiritual consequences. Likewise, those covenants we have with the church are binding and cannot be ignored. Through a covenant relationship, we are accountable to one another and to those who are over us in the Lord.

As Jacob renewed his covenants with God, he experienced a grand awakening of the spiritual priorities in his life. That same reality awaits the humblest of God's children. God honors those who honor their promises to Him.

The **Pain** and the **Glory**

JACOB EXPERIENCED A RADICAL CHANGE

Jacob was never the same after his return to Bethel. He carried with him to his grave the fresh remembrances of a God who never abandons those who are hungry to know Him and who will pay the price to maintain a vibrant relationship with Him. It is also important to note that Jacob's personal renewal brought about a renewal for his entire family. Personal and family renewals could be the beginning of the greatest revival of this century.

Personal renewal will produce some radical changes in the life of the Christian. What are some of the changes we should expect?

■ We will desire to spend more time with God in prayer.

■ We will possess a hunger to know more of God's Word and to devote time daily to that pursuit.

■ We will seek for and rely upon daily quiet time with God in which we think upon His goodness and rehearse His blessings.

■ We will experience worship from a private and public perspective in a manner hardly imagined before.

■ We will actualize Christian service from a perspective of joy and privilege rather than from a sense of duty.

Most of us can identify with the prayer of David in Psalm 51:10—"Create in me a clean heart, O God; and renew a right spirit within me." David knew he had sinned and that he needed forgiveness, but he also knew his needs went beyond forgiveness. He understood that unless there were some radical changes in the way he thought and acted, he would be right back asking God to forgive him for commission of the same sins.

David needed a renovation of his entire mental and moral nature. He needed a renewal brought about by a creative act of God. Forgiveness is required only when there is willful sin, but the need for personal renewal is ever with us. Renewal is as basic to spiritual growth as spring to the rebirth of nature.

Principles
of
Renewal

1
Personal Desperation

2
Listening to God's Voice

3
Putting Away Hindrances

4

Returning to Your Bethel

5

Rebuilding the Altar

6

Renewing Your Vows

7

Experiencing Miraculous Change

"For many years I have believed that if enough individuals become involved in personal renewal, the corporate renewal of the church would be automatic. I no longer believe that."

5

Much More Is Needed

The prophet Ezra understood the importance of personal renewal while also acknowledging the necessity of corporate renewal. After he confessed his own sins and made things right between himself and God, he then confessed the sins of the priests as well as those of the people (Ezra 9:6, 7). What followed is a beautiful example of renewal of an entire community of believers.

> *Now when Ezra had prayed, and when he had confessed, weeping and casting himself down before the house of God, there assembled unto him out of Israel a very great congregation of men and women and children: for the people wept very sore....And they made proclamation*

The **Pain** and the **Glory**

throughout Judah and Jerusalem...that they should gather themselves together unto Jerusalem....And Ezra the priest stood up, and said unto them, Ye have transgressed....Now therefore make confession unto the Lord God of your fathers, and do his pleasure: and separate yourselves from the people of the land....Then all the congregation answered and said with a loud voice, As thou hast said, so must we do (Ezra 10:1, 7, 10-12).

For many years I have believed that if enough individuals become involved in personal renewal, the corporate renewal of the church would be automatic. I no longer believe that. While it is true that the flames of corporate renewal are usually ignited by the glowing embers of personal renewal, this is not automatic. There comes a time when, as in the case of the restoration of Israel, the Body must make a corporate move toward God. This move must be studied and deliberate.

I now have a new vision for renewal in the church. It is a vision in which church leaders confess, repent and cast themselves down before the house of God. They then repent for the transgressions of the Body, issuing a call for the entire community of believers to make a confession unto the Lord and do His pleasure.

When this happens, husbands and wives reach out to each other and to their children, declaring, "Regardless of what the rest of the world does, this house will serve the Lord." Brothers and sisters in the fellowship of believers extend hands to one another, covenanting to be the people of God on earth. The church reaches out to those who have been hurt and offended, offering them healing and comfort. Church leadership makes necessary changes to recapture the vitality of a movement called and commissioned to fulfill God's plan on earth. This is that corporate renewal for which so many have prayed and yearned.

It occurred to me a few years ago that there is a difference in how Church of God members refer to the church. Usually this different perspective is a matter of individual age. Older members are likely to refer to the church as a movement. Younger members call it a denomination. There is no question but what the Church of God began as a dynamic movement of simple but dedicated people, committed to total obedience of God's Word and leadership of the Holy Spirit. What a tragedy it would be for the church to end up in cold and formal institutionalism!

There is nothing inherently evil about institutions. In fact, a movement cannot exist very long without institutions and organizational structures. An institution becomes a very important and vital part of any significant movement. It is when its adherents are more committed to organizational structure than to the living God that institutionalization becomes a threat to the church's existence.

Institutional religion is primarily interested in perpetuating itself rather than creating a free and open atmosphere where people experience a deep move of the Holy Spirit. Institutionalism is more concerned with correctness of structure and policy than quality of life for its adherents or the outreach of its ministry.

The **Pain** and the **Glory**

We must ask ourselves, "Have we moved away from the essence of New Testament Christianity which made us a vital, dynamic movement more than a hundred years ago?" If we have, can we restore those basic principles to our movement, and what must be done?

Eldon Trueblood says in *Your Other Vocation*, "There have been different great steps at different times in Christian history, because one of the most remarkable features of the Christian faith is its ability to reform itself *from the inside*. However vigorous the outside critics of the Church may be, the inside critics, who love the movement which they criticize, are far more vigorous and searching. Reformation is not accidental or exceptional, but characteristic and intrinsic. This crust forms repeatedly, but there is always volcanic power to break through it" (1952, p. 32).

When people question the future of their church, they usually respond in one of four ways:

1. Some give up, abandoning the church for supposedly brighter skies and greener pastures.

2. Some become frustrated, feeling the only way to change things is to tear down the structure and start over.

3. Still others feel trapped, not particularly enticed to leave nor inclined to tear down but bound by a fatalism which says, "My roots are too deeply planted in this church to move, but I have little hope that things are going to change. I'll stay, but I'll not insist nor strongly influence my children to do the same." This last is a tragic alternative, robbing individuals of their heritage and leaving a new generation without roots.

4. Some choose reformation and renewal. This is

the volcanic power from within of which Eldon Trueblood speaks. It says unequivocally, "I am not running away. I am not going to be an anarchist. I am not going to give up my past nor deprive my children of being part of a movement which I believe was begun by God himself. I am going to yield myself as God's instrument to restore the essence of New Testament Christianity to the church."

If we are to avoid or overcome the terrible blight of institutionalism, we must not be afraid of honest probing and prayerful self-appraisal. Some questions we cannot brush aside. We must periodically come face-to-face with our stewardship of the gospel. Whether our programs are successful is not the issue. Pragmatism has never been a scriptural revelation. The real issue is whether or not we will be able to give an adequate witness to our generation. How well are we doing with the mission God has called us to fulfill? How well are we doing with the resources He has given? Improving our programs and our structure is not enough. We need more than better singing and better preaching: We need renewed commitment to mission.

George Santayana the philosopher said, "A nation that does not know history is fated to repeat it." The same could be said about a church. Religious history is replete with stories of how vibrant spiritual awakenings lost their vitality, even ancient Israel.

In the Old Testament it appears that religion was flourishing in Israel. The people were precise in their observance of religious practices. They were able to prevail against much stronger nations because they were favored of God. They were holy people, special to God, and God himself watched out after them.

The **Pain** and the **Glory**

Yet in spite of all of this, Israel lost her vibrant relationship with God. She simply turned from God and started looking after her own affairs. Israel built her own houses and let the house of God lie in ruins. God's basic question to them was "What have I done to deserve this?" He asked in Jeremiah 2:5, "What iniquity have your fathers found in me, that they have gone far from me, and have walked after vanity, and have become vain?" He said in Jeremiah 2:8, "...The pastors also transgressed against me, and the prophets prophesied by Baal, and walked after things that do not profit."

Jeremiah knew the people of God were rushing down a road toward a mournful and catastrophic end. It was his lot in life to stand in their way and try to turn them back. Jeremiah called for reformation, a return to the covenants Israel had made with God, and he assured Israel God was ready to receive her back (Jeremiah 4:12, 13).

Jeremiah did not resort to gimmicks or shortcuts. He relied entirely on the Word of the Lord for reformation. The Word of God must be our guide for renewal as well. The people of God must be a people of the Book. Biblical renewal affects all aspects of our life—devotional, ethics, evangelism, ministry, worship. While biblical renewal is painful, nothing of great consequence will ever be accomplished without someone being willing to suffer. It is easier to chew candy than a steak, but there is no comparison in nutritional value. It may be easier for us to develop our own criteria for renewal, but true spiritual revival is not possible apart from the Word.

At least three things should serve as first-alert danger signals that a church is moving toward institution-

"When church members become more involved in 'church work' than in 'the work of the church,' institutionalization has already set in."

alism.

The first danger signal is an inadequate purpose. When church members become more involved in "church work" than in "the work of the church," institutionalization has already set in. Someone has said if the Holy Spirit were to completely withdraw from some churches, 95 percent of their programs would continue unchanged. If that is true, it is sad commentary on how far some efforts have taken us.

An experience I had at my first pastorate helped focus my attention on the importance of mission above mere activity. The church was more in debt than the few faithful folk had ability to pay, so I resorted to selling doughnuts every week to help with church payments and utilities. At least two and a half days a week were devoted to this well-meant enterprise. One Saturday I walked toward the front door of a home where several children were playing in the yard. As I moved toward the walkway with three dozen doughnuts firmly in hand I thought, *These children should be in Sunday school.* I intended to invite them after I made the sale. When the children saw me they jumped up and ran into the house exclaiming, "Mommy, Mommy, the doughnut man is here."

That was my last week to sell doughnuts. I was determined to be known as a man of God, a preacher, a pastor—anything but a doughnut man. After that we had our greatest growth—financially, spiritually and numerically.

Some pastors and church members are so busy they are near exhaustion. The question that matters is "Are we busy doing what God has called us to do?"

When Lenin met in Moscow with a few of his comrades to discuss overthrow of the government, the Russian clergy is said to have been in a church a few blocks down the street, arguing about the attire priests should wear in the pulpit.

Some issues are vital to our existence. Some are not. As the people of God, we must know the difference.

A second danger against which we must guard is the blight of mediocrity, blood brother and forerunner of apathy. Mediocrity is a concert pianist trying to play Beethoven's Fifth Symphony while using only three notes of an 88-note keyboard. It is a Naval captain using only one gun of a 40-gun battleship when the fleet is under attack. It is a gifted sculptor forming clay pigeons to be shot to pieces in a shooting gallery. Mediocrity is a church that uses its gifts, talents and resources for activities which have no eternal value.

I read several years ago about a school of whales who beached themselves on a sandbar just off the coast of California. For weeks the scientists were baffled. Eventually they determined the whales beached themselves chasing tiny sardines. What a waste of power! The church cannot make the mistake of chasing small priorities.

A third danger that indicates the institutionalization of a church is a lack of sensitivity to the Holy Spirit. The winds of renewal are sweeping across our world. God is doing a great work. People in mainline denominations are opening up to the fullness of the Spirit and His work among men. Gospel doors are opening which have been traditionally closed. If we are to be a viable movement in our world, we cannot sleep through the harvest. We must be a vital part of what the Holy Spirit is doing.

God never intended we should carry on His work for our own purposes or in our own strength. He made provision that we link up with the greatest power and strength this world has known—His Holy Spirit—but we must maintain contact with Him and be sensitive to all He desires to do in our world.

Many challenges face a church that is serious about spiritual renewal. Obviously, a book of this size cannot cover all of them, and I probably do not understand what all these challenges really are. However, I do feel it is important to note a few of what I believe to be our more obvious needs.

WE MUST DEVELOP AND ARTICULATE A SOLID BIBLICAL THEOLOGY

A friend of mine shared that as a young man he was shocked to hear a leading camp meeting preacher say, "I really don't need the Bible to tell me what to believe. I already have all I need forever settled in my heart and mind."

We had *better* care what the Bible says. It is by what "thus saith the Word of the Lord" that we will be judged: not by church *Minutes* or camp meeting sermons or personal convictions, but by the Word of God. It is vital that we commit ourselves to personal study of the Word and that as a movement, we set forth those theological principles which are basic to New Testament discipleship.

There is a growing hunger on the part of ministers and laity alike to genuinely know what the Bible says about issues. Correspondingly, there is an increasing mistrust of ministers and teachers who base the acceptance of their message strictly on an emotional appeal rather than on the Word. People living in a world perched on the precipice of destruction want more than fluff, froth and frivolity. Dying men need a living Word.

In the past few decades we have made great strides toward forming and publishing our theological positions, but we have a ways to go yet. While the whole church world grapples with understanding the *charismata* (gifts of the Spirit), we sit on more than a 100-year heritage. The authority of the baptism of the Holy Spirit—to which we have testified for longer than any other movement—must be assessed and explained clearly through a Pentecostal theology. Testimony to the experience alone is no longer adequate, if it ever was. This world wants and needs theological expositions which stand up to the most critical but honest searcher.

There are also other great doctrines of Scripture to which we must offer a pen of explanation—the doctrine of divine healing, the doctrine of the Kingdom, the doctrine of sanctification and the doctrine of eschatology, to name a few. We will take a giant step toward addressing these vital issues when our theologians are recognized equally with those of charismatic and popular appeal.

WE MUST DEFINE AND COMMIT TO A CLEAR VISION OF OUR MISSION

"Well-meaning programs and lofty plans are meaningless to a church with no vision of mission."

One man recently said about his church, "We are really on the move at our church. Trouble is, we've forgotten where we wanted to go."

Some churches would be better off if they suspended operation for a while, at least until they figured out where they are going. A church with no vision of mission is sinking, and all the best efforts of man will not save it if vision and vitality are not restored. Well-meaning programs and lofty plans are meaningless to a church with no vision of mission. Efforts become acts of sheer futility, tantamount to rearranging the deck chairs on the Titanic.

God has a plan for the church, both as a worldwide Body and as a local fellowship. Church leadership has attempted through Project 2000 to articulate those priorities which prepare us as a worldwide movement to meet the challenges of a twenty-first century. While this is a worthy objective, it means nothing if congregations do not define their community mission and set about with unswerving commitment to fulfill it.

WE MUST CREATE IN OUR MEMBERSHIP A DEEPENING OF THE DEVOTIONAL LIFE

Much has already been said about the need for personal renewal, but it cannot be overstated. No movement is any stronger or weaker than the collective strength or weakness of its adherents. Some have existed for years in the Pentecostal faith, believing they can survive on benefits derived from public proclamation and worship. That's all they have done: existed and survived. God has

The **Pain** and the **Glory**

a spiritual dimension in which believers conquer and triumph. This realm of living is never realized vicariously through another's experiences. It comes only through the crucible of personal encounter and devotion.

Whatever commitments we make to enhance the impact of public worship, let us not overlook the guidance necessary to lead our people into deeper devotional life. Nothing is more powerful in the hands of God than a renewed body of believers.

WE MUST DEMAND AN INTEGRITY OF LEADERSHIP COMMENSURATE WITH NEW TESTAMENT PRINCIPLES

The whole religious world is periodically shaken by shortcomings and betrayals of trusted leaders, men who fail to live up to standards they enunciated for others. Few setbacks are harder to overcome than these blatant failures of people in leadership, for no amount of professionalism, stardom or charismatic ability will compensate for a shoddy life. The underlying principle embraced by most people is "If you don't live it, you don't believe it." We say to our leaders, "If you believe it, live it. If you don't believe it, don't say it."

Even politicians are required to submit to rigid examinations before presenting themselves as candidates for public office. How much more should the body of Christ expect its leaders to be in harmony with the exacting demands of New Testament principles!

WE MUST REDEFINE THE MEANING OF CHURCH MEMBERSHIP

Right now there is genuine confusion as to what constitutes church membership. What does a person have to do to no longer be a member of the Church of God? We say, "Well, that changes from time to time." Indeed it does. The question is, Should it?

Let me give you two examples. I know someone who was disfellowshipped from the church for going to a high school ball game. I know of another man who was convicted of a felony, who served his time in prison, and who returned home without ever being brought to discipline by the church.

I'm not suggesting we get trigger-happy and turn repentant people out of the fellowship. I am suggesting there are circumstances under which individuals forfeit their right to fellowship of the church but, the important thing is, there must be consistency. A person's right to be a member of the church should not depend on the whims or personal preferences of a few people. Only the Body itself, under the direction of the Holy Spirit and under the astute and conscientious guidance of men and women of the Word, has a right to determine what constitutes church membership.

The integrity of the Body itself is threatened when confusion exists over the meaning of membership. Membership must mean something if we are going to encourage our youth and new converts to become part of the fellowship. Becoming a member of a local fellowship of believers is, according to Scripture, an important part of our Christian commitment.

Perhaps the reason so many of our church members cannot be accounted for is that they never really understood to what they were committing themselves in the first place. They have thus drifted away.

Several years ago, while serving as state director of youth and Christian education, I was involved in promoting a Sunday school enlargement campaign in which a grape was affixed to barren branches of a vine every time a newcomer came to class. A serious problem arose in the campaign. The grapes wouldn't stick to the branches. It turns out that the company who printed the campaign did not put the right consistency of glue on the back of the grapes, and heat caused them to fall off. We need a membership disciplined to stick with the church because they know and are committed to those things which the church believes.

WE MUST INVOLVE LAITY IN MINISTRY IN MORE MEANINGFUL WAYS

I have felt for a long time that laity will write the final chapter in the history of the church. If we indeed take the Great Commission of Jesus Christ seriously, there are simply not enough clergy to get the job done. We must rely on our total resources, most of which sit on our pews week after week.

The fact that we have this tremendous, almost untapped, resource available is perhaps reason enough for us to get busy motivating them for more active involvement in the Lord's work, but that fact in itself pales beside the real reason we need a motivated laity. An uninvolved laity will lose its saltiness. A great light will be hidden under a bucket. The tragic result will be millions of people who will never hear of God's grace and mercy if the laity remain silent.

The population explosion of this world is staggering. It took from the beginning of time to 1930 for the world's population to reach the first two billion. It took the next 50 years for the next two billion. At our present growth rate, it will take only 20 years to reach the third two billion, and few people are speculating where we go from there. One thing is certain, if these people are to be reached with the gospel, the church has to enlarge its vision for laborers in the harvest.

WE MUST SEEK FOR CLEARER UNDERSTANDING OF SPIRITUAL GIFTS AND THEIR OPERATION IN THE CHURCH

A few years ago, I wrote an open letter to youth leaders in which I raised a challenging and somewhat controversial issue. I suggested many young people were seriously questioning the operation of the Holy Spirit in the church, almost to the point of mistrust, and that very little positive teaching was addressing the issue. While some improvements have been made, we are still woefully short of training our constituency in understanding the operation of spiritual gifts in the church.

For some reason, we seem afraid to face issues

centering on operation of the gifts of the Holy Spirit, as though concerned about hinting we do not believe in the supernatural. We make a serious mistake if we interpret signs and wonders alone as grounds of faith, approval or power with God. To require authenticity in the operation of spiritual gifts does not mean we are skeptical of the real thing. It means only that we believe there is a real thing. We don't have to settle for a pretense or substitute.

Scriptural criteria are very clear in evaluating spiritual gifts. First, spiritual gifts always testify to the basic Christian confession that "Jesus is Lord" (1 Corinthians 12:3). Second, they always build up the church (1 Corinthians 12:7; Ephesians 4:11, 12). Third, they are governed by love (1 Corinthians 13; Romans 12:9; Ephesians 4:15, 16). Fourth, they are always manifested through sanctified lives that are in harmony with God's Word (Acts 5:32; 1 Peter 1:15, 16; Ephesians 5:25-27).

The church should never be afraid to test spiritual gifts by these scriptural mandates.

WE MUST REEMPHASIZE THE IMPORTANCE OF EVANGELISTIC OUTREACH

Historically, evangelical churches seem to go through alternating periods of fervency and those times in which the emphasis is placed on tuning up the internal machinery. It is not uncommon for churches who once saw as their primary mission the salvation of the lost, and who devoted the major part of their resources and energies

"A church where there are no new births either dies or degenerates into a social order."

to that objective, to become prudent, self-serving and more interested in what goes on in the sanctuary, educational facility or family-life center than in outreach ministries. These churches place a major emphasis on the quality of worship, the level of fellowship among their constituents, and the comfort and convenience of their facilities rather than on new converts. All too many of these churches survive more on biological and transfer growth than on evangelistic results.

While it is obvious the church needs to periodically review and upgrade its ministries and programs, it should never do so at the expense of its evangelistic witness. One does not have to be at the expense of the other. Few things will revitalize the life of the church more than seeing men, women and children brought to a saving knowledge of Jesus Christ. Nothing gives more meaning to the life of the Body than to snatch people from the jaws of hell. A church where there are no new births either dies or degenerates into a social order.

WE MUST REVIEW OUR EMPHASIS ON THE MINISTRY OF TEACHING

When I rise from a reading of the Gospels, the most lasting impression I have of Jesus Christ is that of Master Teacher. When Scripture says, "He opened his mouth, and taught them" (Matthew 5:2), I feel near to the urgency of His message and sensitive to His willingness to share all He is with others. There is perhaps no other area of His life and ministry in which we can more joyfully share than in the ministry of teaching. Teaching puts us in a relationship of actually representing Him to others. What a fantastic privilege!

A pastor in whose church I was a guest shared that none of his young adults attended Sunday school anymore and asked if I had any suggestions. I inquired as to whether he had discussed the matter with his people. He hadn't. With his permission, I requested Sunday lunch at a nearby restaurant with a select group of young adults and asked, "Why don't you attend Sunday school?"

Their response was about as straightforward as my question. One said, "Have you ever heard the teacher?"

"No."

"Well," he said, "if you had, you wouldn't wonder why we don't like Sunday school.

"The teacher is like a *Sunday School Commentary* wired for sound. She usually reads out of the commentary and never has anything relevant to life. Tell the pastor to get us a teacher who will challenge us from the Word, and we'll be back to Sunday school."

A church that does not train and equip teachers to effectively communicate God's Word will soon become another statistic to substantiate the demise of the church's teaching ministry. Worse, we may well produce a generation which doesn't know what God's Word says, let alone how to apply it to daily living.

WE MUST REAFFIRM OUR COMMITMENT TO CHILDREN AND YOUTH

The **Pain** and the **Glory**

How often have we declared, "Our children and our youth are our greatest resource"? Yet, our actions don't always match that declaration.

In a book titled *The Church and Its Youth,* I called for the church to make youth ministry a priority and work of the entire church. I saw then what I thought was a trend toward relegating this vital ministry to a few individuals rather than assuming it was the work of the whole church. I really believe we have made some noticeable strides in this area, but we need more.

A changing economy often forces the church to prioritize its programs and ministries. Economic moves seem always to hit hardest those who pay the bills. If that happens I fear we will see a de-emphasis in this vital area of ministry on the general, state and local levels of ministry. The risk of losing our young people is a price too high to pay. A youth ministry that starts at birth and nurtures our youth through college is absolutely necessary if we are to remain a viable movement in the years approaching the twenty-first century and beyond.

WE MUST CONDUCT PERIODIC REVIEWS OF OUR ECCLESIASTICAL STRUCTURES

It seems almost irreverent to speak of ecclesiastical structures in comparison with some of the other issues raised on preceding pages. However, whether we like it or not, man-made structures *do* have direct bearing on the spiritual well-being of the church.

For more than 100 years, the Church of God has

experienced many changes in its organizational structure. Some were brought about by radical and sometimes disruptive events. Others came about by due process of church polity. The indication seems to be that change will occur. The lesson we can perhaps learn is that we must always be open to making those necessary structural changes and must not fear placing them before the entire body for decision as to what is best.

Any movement or organization so bound to the past that orderly changes in structure cannot be affected is in danger of anarchy and extinction. It is essential that we periodically look at what we are doing in light of Scripture. If any scriptural principle is being violated, we have to change. We have no choice.

We need also to review what we are doing in light of utilizing the best possible methods of sound stewardship management and the best possible organizational structure. Organizational structures do not exist to serve the few who are in positions of leadership. They must serve the whole body or they are inherently wrong.

CONCLUSION

One of my favorite childhood stories was about a king hoaxed by traveling salesmen into buying magical yarn only intelligent people could see. Not wanting to appear unintelligent, the king purchased the yarn and commanded his tailors to weave it into fabric and to fashion him a new robe.

Word spread throughout the kingdom. The king

was going to wear his beautiful new robe in a parade so all his subjects could behold its magnificence. Of course, they were all warned that only intelligent people could see the robe.

Everything went well until one little boy, more concerned with honesty than with pseudo-intelligence, yelled out, "The king has no clothes."

Everyone began laughing, pointing at the king, chanting in unison, "The king has no clothes."

The king ran for cover.

Truth is sometimes difficult to face. Often we prefer to believe a lie than to appear negative or to risk being perceived as unintelligent. Positive change will never come to those who will not honestly face the truth of present conditions. If we are content to agree tongue-in-cheek that all is well when deep in our hearts we know better, we can never be instruments of renewal. God demands first of all that we be honest with Him.

Today as a church we desperately need to see ourselves as God sees us.

Is it possible that we have become so preoccupied with goals of institutional maintenance that we are quenching the Holy Spirit? Are we so caught up in our own agendas that we cannot hear the painful cry of brothers and sisters who are in need of love and empathetic care? Are we so busy doing church work that we cannot sense the agony of a world that is blundering its way straight into hell? Is it possible we are still clinging to the old visions and past accomplishments when God is trying to break through with fresh revelation of His love and power?

Often it takes a radical shaking to awaken the church to its ministry and mission. The shaking has begun. It is not a mild tremor. It is an earthquake of major proportions. We hardly get ourselves braced from the aftershock of the last quake until another one is on its way.

In the midst of this purging,

...will there be those who turn aside to see a burning bush?

...who choose voluntarily to suffer the reproach of God's people?

...or who wrestle all night with One who alone can put matters in proper perspective?

Our future as a denomination is as bright as the promises of God...or as dark as this world's plight.

The choice is ours. God is leading His church back to its roots of purity and *back* to its commitment to ministry and mission.

To resist this move of His Holy Spirit is to assign ourselves to an insignificant role in the last-day revival. Positive change will not come easily. Renewal is costly, and we alone determine whether we are willing to pay God's price.

There can be no more running from the pain. The glory of God's promises comes only with the agony of His refinement.

The pain may cut deep...but Christ's promised glory is incredible!

Principles
of
Renewal

1
Solid Bible Theology

2
Clear Vision of Mission

3
Attention to Devotional Life

4
Integrity of Leadership

5
Definition of Church Membership

6
Development of Lay Ministry

7
Clearer Understanding of Spiritual Gifts

8
Renewed Emphasis on Evangelistic Outreach

9
New Emphasis on Teaching

10
Commitment to Children and Youth

11
Periodic Reviews of the Ecclesiastical Structure

Sources

Barclay, William. *The All-Sufficient Christ*. Philadelphia: The Westminster Press, 1963.

Baxter, Richard. *The Reformed Pastor*. Portland, Oregon: Multnomah Press, 1982.

Briscoe, Stuart. *How to Be a Motivated Christian*. Wheaton, Illinois: Victor Books, 1987.

Bounds, E. M. *Power Through Prayer*. Grand Rapids, Michigan: Baker Book House, 1986.

Brueggemann, Walter. *Hopeful Imagination*. Philadephia: Fortress Press, 1986.

Christenson, Larry. *Welcome Holy Spirit*. Minneapolis: Augsburg Publishing House, 1987.

Foster, Richard J. *Celebration of Discipline*. San Francisco, Harper & Row, 1978.

Harvey, Van A. *A Handbook of Theological Terms*. New York: MacMillian Publishers, 1979.

MacDonald, Gordon M. *Restoring Your Spiritual Passion*. Nashville, Tennessee: Oliver Nelson, 1986.

Mallone, George. *Furnace of Renewal*. Illinois: Inter-
Varsity Christian Fellowship, 1981.

Oswalt, John. *Where Are You,God?* Wheaton, Illinois:
Victor Books, 1982.

Palms, Roger C. *First Things First*. Wheaton, Illinois:
Victor Books, 1983.

Pinnock, Clark H. *Three Keys to Spiritual Renewal*.
Minneapolis, Minnesota: Bethany House
Publishers, 1985.

Ravenhill, Leonard. *Why Revival Tarries*. Minneapolis,
Minnesota: Bethany House Publishers, 1959.

Shaller, Lyle E. *It's a Different World*. Nashville,
Tennessee: Abingdon Press, 1987.

Shoemaker, Sam. *Extraordinary Living for Ordinary
Men*. Grand Rapids, Michigan: Zondervan
Publishing House, 1965.

Swindoll, Charles. *Strike the Original Match*. Portland,
Oregon: Multnomah Press, 1980.

"The Fall of Jimmy Swaggart." *People Weekly*.
March 7, 1988.

Trueblood, Eldon. *Your Other Vocation*. New York:
Harper & Brothers, 1952.

Watson, David. *I Believe in the Church*. London: Hodder & Stoughton, 1978.

Worrell, George E. *Resources for Renewal*. Nashville, Tennessee: Broadman Press, 1975.

———————————

Review Questions

Chapter 1

1. How have spiritual renewals in the church been sparked in the past?
2. What are five prerequisites to spiritual renewal?
3. What was the first principle adopted by early members of the Church of God?
4. What is the primary mission or challenge of the church?

Chapter 2

1. What is a Christian's most powerful source of hope?
2. What is the meaning of the word *apathy*?
3. What are four results of apathy?
4. According to the author, what has been the secret of the church's extraordinary fellowship?

Chapter 3

1. What is Paul's prayer for believers in Ephesians 1:17, 18?
2. What are "the three terrible R's" of traditionalism?
3. What are five beneficial results of experiencing re-

newal of concepts?

4. In the author's account of the Indian man who wanted to join the church, what had the man discovered about the mission of the church by reading the book of Acts?

Chapter 4

1. What were Jacob's seven steps to personal renewal?
2. In what ways do Christians today hear the voice of God?
3. What are some examples of hindrances to spiritual life?
4. What is the meaning of the biblical name "El-beth-el"?
5. What changes might a person expect who has experienced radical personal spiritual renewal?

Chapter 5

1. What is the author's "new vision for renewal in the church"?
2. What are three signs that a church is becoming institutionalized?
3. What are eleven needs of the church in order for it to experience renewal?

————————————

NOTES

NOTES

NOTES

NOTES